THE
TRIPPING SPRIGGAN

First published by
Psychedelic Press & Breaking Convention
Falmouth, Cornwall

ISBN: 978-0992808846

Printed in Cornwall, United Kingdom

For more information:
psychedelicpress.co.uk
breakingconvention.co.uk

CONTENT

INTRODUCTION

By Robert Dickins

The psychedelic journey through literature is often a rather static affair that needs pre-designed maps to navigate, filled as it's been with archaic cartographies of the psyche.

It certainly doesn't help when someone, some time ago, decided it was near identical with the mystical experience, and was therefore 'ineffable' – not much of a starting point for prose writers. Poets, on the other hand, long after the ineffable – it is the experiential fodder with which they seem ideally placed to dance with.

Language is transient and flows for the poet. It describes through context, feeling, form and emotion; it gives impression and is impressed by the reader. The dictionary is an archaic guide to be interpreted, not a pedant's hammer used to fix meaning into shape – to prove some unrelated point. The poet and the tripper, unfixed and free, are fellows of the Altered State, in ways the prose writer often isn't.

So, when I was approached by the wonderful Breaking Convention crew about producing a publication for 2015's event – the 3rd International Conference on Psychedelic Consciousness – it was obvious that some poetical madness would be the perfect trip for those in attendance.

We've had numerous wonderful contributions that have gone to make up this anthology of poetry, which is centred on altered states of experience and consciousness. There's a strong thread of psychedelia, and a reoccurring, thematic concern with the world of Fey; self-transforming I'm told is the way.

The Tripping Spriggan is a journey through transient states, as much about past experiences as it is about present poetics, and I hope you enjoy taking this journey with us.

HIGH, KEW

By Andy Roberts

Plant genitals, tree porn
Fertilize my mind
Must I leave this fertile ground?

THE ELVEN KING

By Frank Dietrich

Some say they've seen the Elven King,
Some say he's no more than a tale,
I once did meet the Elven King
In the northern forest, in the greenest vale.

He was clad in clothes as green as leaves
And his cloak was grey and light and I said:
'Where did you get your fine grey coat from?'
– 'From the old willow's waving head.'

So we sat by a stone and drank his wine
that tasted strange and sweet and I said:
'Where did you get your sweet red wine from?'
– 'From the woodberries so dark and red.'

Anon there came his five young daughters
And they danced around in a ring and I said:
'Where did your five young daughters come from?'
– 'From the wild roses' mossy bed.'

And then he took a pouch from his vest
And showed me three golden coins and I said:
'Where did you get your coins of gold from?'
– The Elven King, he dropped down dead.

TO THE FORE

By Kripi Malviya

Giddy as fractals from
My kaleidoscopical eyes
I wait, pretend, prolong, push

For not a place
And definitely not a human
And not just for desolation, despair or ecstasy
But for an empty stomach half broken glass of white
noise,
An intricate study of how pebbles are stones,
Split ends, the smell of your day old breath,
Concentrated 'dhyaan' of broken skin

For making sense of fear
But not making any sense at all
For lucid lies of art,
And forgotten senses emerging
That mock all realisations

For the luxury of written hurt
For spontaneous sleep;
Elusive like a drunken dream

For the convulsing sob of time passing
For every now that has ever been
For every now that has never been

THE CUTLASS GNOMES OF CUT-GLASS HOMES SANG EULOGIES FOR ME

By Castapopoulos the young

I met the elves; the tales are true,
They spoke to me with tails of blue,
And green upon their shim'rin' eyes,
And slyness on their faerie smiles,
And clockwork lockets full of mud,
And patchwork pockets black with blood,
With words that came in noiseless floods,
And when they danced they danced with gods,
And one such god was me.

I asked the elves where they called home,
They said that all roads lead to Rome,
All time is now and all place here,
And then they laughed and disappeared,
And in their place came rocking-chairs,
And twelve-eyed weasels all in pairs,
And putrid lights and oblong airs,
And all things come to he who dares,
But I did not dare to see.

13

The airs gave way to sing-song night,
And in the dark I missed the sprites,
Who waltzed with me in engine halls,
In motor pools and grinding stalls,
Who sleep down deep in eyelid walls,
With mantis guards and bloodshot dolls,
Beyond the geometric malls,
O', my memory, far too small;
Their faces I could not recall,
Would they remember me?

SAFE-PROOFING

By Toby Slater

Out of my mind into daylight,
From bone rooms to new morning.

Cold tiles pave to an open door,
The picture-book's pages turn.

Birds trill in call-and-response,
A crescendo in empty sky.

Smoking breath and shadows
On the path that marks time.

Verdant gardens glisten -
With crystal crunch underfoot.

I will not carry a begging bowl,
Nor will I cave to the sucker punch.

I am safe-proofing while reaching up
To paint the walls of the temple -

With a groan, a croon or a sigh it is done.

Into The Ether

By Matthew Nash

All manner of potted plants
Were scattered across the room,
The walls animate, dancing with licks of candlelight.
An arm stretched back to our rituals of old,
A sacrament to all that is right.
An opening of the mind's eye
And what are we but our minds?
An expansion of ourselves
A tale engraved since ancient times.
In a landscape made of jewels
More precious than any stone
An ever changing image
That only I can see, alone.
For if all we are as beings,
Is nothing more than our thoughts.
Then within my mind I shall roam
In psychedelic courts.
I have no quarrel with my waking state
Or how I view the world by day
But a voyage into the ether
Can forever change the game.

UNTITLED

By Billy Merrick

I love you with my hatred,
So please hate my love,
If the puddles were so sacred,
How rotten were the doves,
Who flew upon your own sky,
Whilst fleeing from above,
On all the borrowing ivy's,
That dressed you in mud,
Twisted twisted sister,
How wicked are they,
Who sipped among the old well,
But scurried as a flea,
Down down we fell, down down I sank
In waters never there,
Swim again
In waters never there.

PEYOTE QUICK-DRAW

By Phil Breach

They meet at Loco Cave, the thieves and bandits,
The picaroons and gila-men and ghouls.
This lethal game they play is sacred, and it's
Called Peyote Quick-draw (Trickster's Rules).

A hefty crop of cactus each consumes,
Guzzled down with swigs of sasparilla.
They wait until the gloaming desert blooms,
Then commence the draw to winnow killed from killer.

For one, the pistol barrel loops around
With sorrowed mouth that spills a sparkling drool.
The other's eyes are anchored at the ground,
Where spiny elementals writhe and mewl.

At last though, the one soothes his sobbing Colt,
And takes aim through the deluge of peyote.
The other slips his moorings with a jolt;
Another sunder'd soul to old Coyote.

An Hallucinogenic Limerick Of Wish Fulfilment

By Ben Sessa

There once was a doctor called Sessa
Whose work was a bit of a stressor.
To undo his tension and augment his pension
He resolved to become a professor.

He knew just the subject to study,
So he called on his infamous buddy:
Along came Prof Nutt who said, 'You're in luck!
But where will we find that much money?'

The costs they faced were distressing,
And the project was barely progressing,
Then Beckley and MAPS came forth with the cash,
And the ethical board gave their blessing.

The illness they wished to extinguish,
And pathological pathway distinguish,
Was commonly seen as P.T.S.D.,
Which they now set their sights to relinquish.

They sat down and starting their planning,
And prayed for no government banning.
They hoped to display, when they gave MDMA,
That Vets' brains would light up with their scanning.

In presenting modus operandi
The media's help came in handy.
The public was ready, the mood it was heady,
The soldiers queued up for their Mandy.

The results when they came were prodigious,
With significance far from litigious.
PTSD was improved, MDMA got approved,
And the project was labeled prestigious.

Psychedelic research saw extension,
New compounds got further attention:
Cannabis, DMT, Psilo, Ket, LSD,
Were the subjects of Breaking Convention.

PSONNET

By Peter Kahn

No truth lies in any drop
Once you start you never stop
Open eyes do not mean love
Left with nothing left to prove
Visions of god have cataracts
Lost in faded cathartic acts
Reality wears a cold disguise
Most old men are not so wise
Brain hangs heavy like drunkard's paunch
A nuclear bomb without key to launch
Blottered reason like logic's tomb
Crammed inside this empty room
All these poems with their blessings shout
But let us cast some healthy doubt

WANDERING SOULS
OF THE NORTH WOOD

By Scott Halperin

The seasons change before your eyes
As summer fades and autumn falls
Leaves from the same tree
Begin to pile around you
As you sit and idly chat
In a forest with your buddy
Tingling toes pick you up
Seeming to take you
Where you're meant
To go

And the mossy ground flows up the trees
And the branches wave in the breeze
And the sun sets in the west

The fiery orange sky fades to pinks and purples
Last light is left shimmering over the lake
The trees grow taller as the sky is vast
Beginning to show its first stars
In this last light you feel
Like perhaps the show in the sky
That golden sunset that melted

Into the lake was something truly
Special and now a blue heron
Swoops low into the water
And your buddy says,
'whoa, was that a fucking pterodactyl?'
And after laughing for possibly
5 seconds or 10 minutes
You casually reply
'I think so.'

THE SONG OF SUSANNA

By Susanna Lafond

I am daughter of man
I am mother of man
I am grandmother of men
I am shapeshifter
I am warrior
I am priestess
I am director
I am actor
I am dancer
I am lover
I am beloved
I am whore
I am muse
I am solitary
I am SHE

Magic Mushrooms

By Joe Loughlin

Dry them, cook them, eat them raw
Gobble down the spores, then eat some more

They taste like shit but they warp your brain
For a few hours you'll become insane

Your head starts to spin – perception change
Enter a new world, magical and strange

Legs start to wobble, laughing and grinning
Colours are vivid, the adventure is beginning!

Then sky's a splash of colours, the moons a swirling crescent
The psychedelic wonders, of nature's little present

Close your eyes and see a kaleidoscope
Your emotions erupting – love, joy and hope

The world as you see it doesn't look straight
Your tripping your tits off, you can't work a gate

A road becomes a river as the trip starts to peak
Your giggling so much that you can barely speak

Outlook altered, embrace the tripping
This time tomorrow, we'll do some more picking!

VOICES OF THE LAND

By Nikki Wyrd

We are the voices
Between the worlds
Listen to our secrets
As time unfurls
We tell of understanding
That future place
Of making the land
A green and living space
As you lie upon the surface
Listen to the worlds below
Hear the voices calling
Shouting Yes! You know!
Use all of your senses
The patterns to find
Use all of your Art
To keep them in mind
Listen deep down
Listen with your bones
Your body is the ground
Your spirit not alone
Listen to the Land
In the dead of night
Hear the rhythm of rain
Hit the drumskin tight
This is a powerful plea

A statement of intent
The people of the earth
Can hear what we meant.

In ages past
When stone was new
We spoke of circles
Of tribes so true
We sang of the sky
With moon stars and sun
We painted pictures
With hands and tongue
The hunt for plants and homes
The quest for life and love
Skills of hearth and harvest
Did not come from above
This world you stand on
And trample underfoot
Is the fount of wisdom
Water Earth Air Wood
Look into the Fire
Feel the heat within your heart
Aware of how you hold your body
Scent the path from where you start

Each time that people sing
Get together in a ring
We call our learning out loud
To those who listen in the crowd.

THE LAUGHING GAS OF LIFE

By Ffion Reynolds

My hysterical hurrah's nest
Is entered again.
And I realise I am in a mess.
Instead of floating on water
I dive deep to the colour:

The fabric of the fabricator.

Like a dream,
I touch and believe it is reality
But the waking to life's lie factory
Is literally media-media in mortality.
In every memory its metaphysics is
Like a drunk olfactory of smells,
So I turn to nirvana.

This apparent higher state says Buddha
My soul is freed from desires
And the Nitrous oxide character of my mind
Sends signals of exhilaration
To every living karma.

WHICH DR WISDOM

By Martin 1Wheel

At Breaking Convention, with a variety of intentions,
We'd gathered from all across the land.
We'd decided you see, that it was time that we
Took this psychedelic matter in hand.
With mixed up emotions, we talked about potions,
Of Entheogens that we knew,
Of chemicals and wonderous herbs
And what goes into the Ayahuasca they brew,
Of Yage and Yopo or Caapi and Viridis,
Or Chagrapanga, Chacruna and Toloache
Should you prefer this,
Of therianthropes and jaguar shaman,
And the songs that they sing at the ceremonies when
They've dosed you or fleeced you,
You'll know which it is,
Cos this Ayahuasca tourism has become very big biz.

With each conversation with folk from all nations,
I totally engaged my sense of facination,
Of 5HT2A and aliens grey,
I found each conversation captivating each day,
Of drug policy and the way that it's changing,
Of MDMA and how it's rearranging.
Those poor soldiers mind's, those with PTSD,
Goodness Rick Doblin's even nearly convinced

The American military,
3/4 methylenedioxy-n-methamphetamine,
E, shrooms or weed,
As we talked we realised we shared a similar creed.
Dr Passie, I'm sure found
my naughty question transparent,
I'm sure he knew I was joking,
I'm sure it was apparent,
When over to Dr Simon Brandt from Liverpool I went,
When he told me about Steven Barker
from Cottonwood
I knew why I'd been sent.
You see the drugs in my head, those naturally there,
Whenever I haven't slept, well they're driving me
spare,
I wish to know, as it seems apparent to me,
That my madness is caused by endogenous DMT

FOUR ON A TRIP

By Graeme Hartley

Outdoors in inner-space
Grey slate-cliff streaked
With blood red trace.
Welsh wind and seaspray, peppering my face.
Internal warmth sends more Acid-shiver
As the air and the shingle
Shimmer and slither.
Four on a trip, at Carmel Head
Four on a trip, and A has just said
'that dose that I gave you was twice the amount.'
As we shake with amusement
The weather grows savage
And the skies even darker
The rain soaks right through
Several layers of parka.
But we're peaking right then
And it can't stop us grinning
And so once again
Psychedelics are winning.
After driftwood and sea glass
Are picked up and sorted
And the trip carries on
To be later reported.

INVISIBLE BORDERS

By Scott Wozniak

Paths unfold
In darkness
As reality
Loosens
Its grip
And wings spread
Unencumbered
By the heretic
Abolishment
Of nature's gift.

Invisible borders
Begin to glow
As we step over
Them, and explore
New lands.

The outer reaches
Of inner space
Stretch
Across galaxies
On elevated
LSD
Mind states
Illuminating

Eternity's
Secret
Resting place.

SITTING STONED ON A SEASIDE STONE

By Joey Connolly

Stoned to the bone my skinny hips
Rest uneasy on a coral rock
Locally grown cannabis sown
No boats at all moored at the dock
Pacific trade winds gently blow
My mind at ease on THCs
Watching the tide ebb and flow
Plumeria scents the soft breeze
Doggerel rap comes out my trap
Rhyming and timing all in play
Coconut crabs draw a sand map
Up and around the beach all day
For today I have all I need
Fresh coconut milk and some weed

D&D

By Gary Bains

…and after an hour I was awake,
The tears of the sun had cried the night away,
I melted into the grass, the river was a rush of glass,
That was when I became…

Deranged and derailed,
Strange trails and the colour prevailed,

I lay in a field all night,
Stars spin and ignite daylight,
Bees sing and the trees exhale,

I was deranged and derailed,

I'd 'ran away' when I was young,
Strawberries, Ohms and California Suns,
I remember a flash in the dark, I remember the time
warp,
And the day that brought on perfect change,

I was deranged and derailed,
Words failed but the colour prevailed,

I'd had a hundred trips,
But I'd never seen the world like this,

Infinite depth in detail,

I was deranged and derailed,

I am as green as the breeze,
I'm as blue as the trees,
I've fallen and I have risen,
I've seen the colour prevail,

...when I was deranged and derailed.

DIVINED FRUIT

By Robert Dickins

Autumn Goddess has
Wet feet and eyes to the floor.
Dew soaked liberty.

Dried on newspaper,
Stories to fit in boxes
With conical gold.

Tuned via light-waves.
Distracted concentration
Atop slowed, stoned Ohms.

Sun rises, mind quiets.
There, perceived, the caps hidden
In blades of fortune.

The Goddess returns.
Mist drapes over her meadow
And the day bears fruit.

ANOTHER POLE, CAT

By John Pickering

From East to West,
There's another pole,
Unmapped by cartography.
Wild mystery
And history,
Endlessly changing
And struggling,
Across time's
Long topography --
Life's
Incredible
Diversity.

Hey, Cat, free yourself.
Exit your inside bubble.
Give the outside troll
Her helpfull toll;
Leave behind
Your pocket's
Digital unimagination.
Explore and discover,
Look and listen,
Poke and smell.
Think what and why.
Learn when, where,

And how.
Now, who will you tell?
Will you get in trouble
If you find
And share
New secrets?
No.
But your mind
Will fly
So exceedingly,
Excitingly well.

PERPETUA

By James Hypheris

Upon solar approach
Time has been eaten
New vector in flames
Burning white jetroar
Mainlining leonine vortices
Hypercalculatory ebb and flow
And flux
And structuring of now and no
Bending shadows to
Frame the photo-
Synthesis of symbiosis
I, plant, plant my feet in
Deep below the plane of soil and
Growth and life
Grimoire geology
Erosion technology
East of the altar
The white seemed holy
But black and green
Held it aloft

PIXIE

By Cameron Adams

Lost in a dark wood,
Reverberations of repercussions
resounding unrepentantly,
The echo of my mind presenting itself as reality.
Illusion, maya, the veil as projection
screen for my thoughts.

I met a pixie.
She pulled aside the screen
And my projections vanished
Into the clearing beyond.

There we danced,
The echo chamber of my mind overcome
As the walls fall away to the refrain 'open, open'.
We dance in spiralling circuits
To glimmering waves of cosmic joy.

A path opens in the wood
I don't know where it goes
But for a while I will walk there
With the pixie.

THE COSMIC JOKER

By Niall Doherty

All of this existence is one big charade
One being, many masks, in majestic parade
And this being has become quite delirious
As in our folly we took ourselves too serious
Time is rendered obsolete the eternal is made manifest
All of life one joyous jape the cosmic joker jibes in jest
And the lesson learned and cherished hereafter
Should be to smile often and delight in laughter.

BEYOND THE DOOR

By Jennie Evangelista-Cruz

Now, I am here
In a land, greeted with warm hugs and smiles
I see the other side,
the world beyond the power of words
Where secrets become truth
Where beauty shines
not from the surface but deep within
Where there is no boundary and everything is free
Where limitations become endless possibilities
Where everything is burning, bleeding,
breathing as one
Like falling in love for the first time…

And I am here
Transported by your light
You give me a little place to sleep
For the rest,
I am happy
I am complete

THE TIM LEARY SCENE

By LiZ Elliot

The Tim Leary Scene
Is Sci-Fi and high
On LSD we fly above the sky.
See the blue ball of Earth,
The birth of stars.
Neurons buzzing, pulsars pulsing,
Waltzing, prancing, twinkling through the cosmos `
Jokers all!

Free fall,
Free love ~ I'm not alone!
Nose cone,
Fish bowl, console ~
It's space-ace Tim
I'm in love with him!
He's brave and full of glory.
Quick-silver fast we view the past
And future story.
All's hunky-dory.
Love and LSD
Some for you, some more for me...

Damn it! We've got to escape this planet!
Fund war no more!
There's worlds galore

For us to explore ~
We've got the know-how
Why don't we go now?

(*Switzerland, 1971*)

NOTHING IS LOST

By Samuel Lascelles Davidson

Roll away, far away, and further
On waves and wings, out-chase the racing weather
Stay-at-homes will fade away and wither
And all their wasted moments come to nothing
Nor will this mean much to me come summer
Not that I would ask to lose you, only
Aren't you more myself than I was ever?

Who's Painting My Dream

By Bruce Rimell

She knows
I am not the artist
But the conduit…

My eyes are her brush,
My body her paint
Dissolving into her visions…

Who she is,
She tells me
And I still do not know…